McDougal, Littell

Teaching and Evaluating
Student Writing

McDougal, Littell & Company

Evanston, Illinois

New York   Dallas   Sacramento

This report was researched and prepared by
Mary Ann Trost, teacher, East Cleveland City Schools
and the editorial staff of McDougal, Littell & Company.

ISBN: 0-86609-473-3

86 87 88 / 12 11 10 9 8 7 6 5 4 3

Contents

Teaching and Evaluating
Student Writing

Writing Instruction Today

Educators know that it is time we took an objective, critical look at writing instruction in our schools. Despite constant and concentrated efforts by teachers to teach composition and the related skills of grammar, usage, and mechanics, student writing has not been improving. In fact, according to Donald Murray, a noted authority on student writing, "Most American high school graduates do not know how to write. This is one of the few statements on which most educators agree, and it is an opinion they share with employers and parents. Writing—the vital ability to express one's self with clarity and grace—is not taught in our schools" (Murray 1968).

Hard-working teachers have a right to feel frustrated. But they also have a right to know where the weaknesses in present writing instruction lie, and what can be done to promote positive change. Teachers want to know: What methods for teaching writing *will* work?

Individuals and groups have been researching the teaching of composition to discover the answer to that question. Among the most respected of these researchers are the following:

1. Donald Graves, professor of Education at the University of New Hampshire. Professor Graves is the author of several books and articles concerning the process of writing and the process-conference approach to its teaching. He has held the positions of teacher, school principal, and language supervisor. At present, Donald Graves is research editor of the magazine *Language Arts*.

2. Donald Murray, professor of English at the University of New Hampshire. In his book *A Writer Teaches Writing*, Murray first analyzes the process by which a writer writes, and then applies the techniques of that process to writing instruction. In addition, Murray has directed the New England School Development Council's Project WRITE and has taught a NESDEC course in the teaching of writing for English teachers. A Pulitzer Prize winner, Murray is the author of several other books and articles in various magazines and professional journals.

3. Shirley Haley-James. Dr. Haley-James is a professor of Language Arts and Reading Education at Georgia State University in Atlanta, Georgia. She has served on the Board of Directors of the National Council of Teachers of English and has chaired committees on teaching written composition. Dedicated to improving student writing, Dr. Haley-James is the author of numerous articles in professional journals.

4. The National Writing Project (formerly known as the Bay Area Writing Project) is a program for staff instruction in the teaching of writing. It has been enormously successful in California and is a prototype for other such programs across the country. Author Jack Hailey, cited below, summarizes the philosophy and techniques of the project.

What Are the Problems?

According to the experts, the reasons why students are not writing well are varied. Donald Graves, after analyzing eight series of language arts texts, has concluded that one of the reasons students can't write is that their texts and their teachers, by and large, ignore the *process* of writing—the method of thinking and revising that must be a part of any successful composing experience (Graves 1977). James Britton, noted English writing authority, has also deplored the misplaced emphasis on the final written product over the process which produced it. He believes that there is "a tendency to value good formulation of some piece of information, but the more important consideration, as far as learning is concerned, is the *ability* to formulate, and not the formulation."

Another reason for poor writing performance may be that many students are not given adequate instruction or practice in composition. According to a 1979 National Association of Educational Progress survey of twenty-six thousand seventeen-year-olds, eighty percent spent less than one-third of their English class time in studying writing (Brown 1983). In another recent study, Arthur N. Applebee, associate professor of Education at Stanford University, reported that, in observed secondary school classrooms, only three percent of the total class time of ninth and eleventh grade pupils was devoted to writing one or more paragraphs, and only three percent of homework assignments required that students write at least one paragraph ("Newsfront" 1981). Donald Murray has summarized the problem this way: "Most students pass through twelve years of English courses, but few students ever have an intensive, concentrated opportunity to write" (Murray 1968).

Other authorities have suggested that writing is not presented in a way that helps students see its value and purpose. For example, writing is seldom used as a tool for discovery and learning. After extensive research in English schools, James Britton concluded that writing was "basically used not as a means of learning but as a way of helping the teachers find out what the kid had learned" (Rosen 1978). Thus, students are prevented from experiencing the communicative and creative power of writing. They lose their motivation to work at writing when writing is reduced to a stale exercise in which they tell the teacher what the teacher already knows.

Finally, experts maintain that even though teachers would like to teach writing, they simply have not had the opportunity to learn how to do so. Studies by Donald Graves and others have shown that in many major universities, courses on the teaching of writing are rare or nonexistent (Graves, 1978). Obviously, instruction in the teaching of writing has not been given high priority in our teacher training.

Improving the Teaching of Writing

Despite these rather discouraging findings, enthusiastic writing experts are convinced that the state of writing instruction *can* be improved. Rexford Brown, director of publications for the Education Commission of the States, has said, "If the bad news is that writing is not faring as well as we'd like, the good news is that it is not really being taught. *Imagine what would happen if we began to teach writing*" (Brown 1983).

This statement, while subtly humorous, is also encouraging. It says that there *is* something we can do about writing instruction in our schools. In order to determine how the teaching of writing can be improved, however, it is first essential to know 1) what writing is and 2) that there is a *process* a writer goes through when he or she writes—a process of thinking, rethinking, writing, and revising.

What Is Writing?

The primary and most exciting aspect of writing has always been that writing is *communication*. Through writing, an individual can reach across space and time to instruct, to entertain, and to touch others. Writing is a powerful way of sharing ideas and feelings.

Secondly, writing is a means of clarifying and discovering what we think. Writing brings vague ideas and emotions into focus and forces the writer to examine these ideas logically and critically. It exposes gaps in knowledge and weaknesses in understanding, pointing out to the writer where his or her thoughts need clarification (Dyson 1982). Unexpected insights and related ideas are also uncovered (Murray 1978). It is this aspect of writing—its role in helping us understand our own thoughts—that makes it invaluable, especially in education. As Richard L. Larson, Associate Dean of Education at Herbert Lehman College, said, "The power of making discoveries—of drawing connections between bits of experience so that they reveal or point to new ideas and problems . . . is . . . one of the powers that makes education possible" (Murray 1978).

The Process of Writing

As stated before, there is a tendency among both educators and writers to view writing in terms of a final product rather than as an ongoing process. Inexperienced writers in particular often believe that writing is the ability to produce well-developed, well-organized ideas as soon as one sets pen to paper. They may expect their first attempt at recording their ideas to be the final product. Experienced writers, on the other hand, know that writing is a cycle of planning, writing, and revising which usually leads to more planning, writing, and revising (Graves 1978; Murray 1968; Hailey; Gaskins; Haley-James[2]; and others). It is a thinking process, a means of first finding out what we want to say, and then deciding on the best way to present it by writing and reworking the writing until we are satisfied with the result.

Students of writing must learn to understand and use such a process. They must be given a pattern to follow that "duplicates in slow motion the steps taken swiftly and naturally by competent writers when they address themselves to any prose composition" (Murray 1968). This can be done, in rough form, by breaking the process of writing into three main stages: Pre-Writing, Writing the First Draft, and Revising. A summary of these stages is given below.

Pre-Writing

The pre-writing stage can also be called the planning stage. It is one of the most basic and essential parts of the writing process (Boiarsky 1982). The purposes of the pre-writing stage are to explore possibilities for topics and presentation, and to begin gathering and organizing the details that will be used to develop the main idea. Writers should complete the following pre-writing steps every time they write:

1. Choose and narrow a topic.
2. Decide on the purpose for writing.
3. Identify the audience who will read the final version.
4. Gather details that develop the topic and suit the purpose and the audience.
5. Put the ideas into a logical order.

Writers should also realize that these plans are merely the first tentative attempts to define and organize ideas. The ideas can be modified slightly or changed drastically at any point in the writing process from pre-writing to the final draft.

Writing the First Draft

The purpose of a first draft is basically to get some ideas down on paper. Even as they work on this draft, which has also been called the "discovery draft," writers often find that they are developing new ideas and refining others. This may necessitate a return to the pre-writing stage to reevaluate other aspects of the writing, such as organization, the choice of supporting details, or even the topic itself. A first draft, therefore, is simply a first attempt by the writer to find out what he or she wants to say. Every writer should be prepared to work through several versions of any piece of writing before reaching a final product.

Errors in grammar, usage, and mechanics should not be a concern at this critical point in the writing process. Worry about such errors only diverts the writer's energy from the discovery and refinement of ideas. There will be time to concentrate on these more mechanical details later, during the revision process.

Rewriting, or Revising

Some writers make the mistake of equating revision with proofreading. Although checking for errors in grammar, usage, and mechanics is important, the greatest part of revising time should actually be spent on content. As previously noted, the first draft of a piece of writing is primarily a way of discovering the ideas that are to be used. The most crucial part of writing occurs on successive drafts, during the revision process.

When revising, a writer should do the following:

1. Check to see that all ideas and details are related to the topic and purpose.
2. Refine good ideas, and add any new ones that could improve the writing.
3. Make certain that the purpose of the paper is clear, and that the content of the writing suits that purpose.
4. Refine the organization of the ideas.
5. Check to see that each sentence flows smoothly to the next.

6. Make sure that the language and content are suitable for the audience.
7. Substitute precise, vivid words for vague language.
8. Proofread for errors in grammar, usage, and mechanics.

It must be pointed out that revision can take place at any time during the writing process. Revision may even require a return to the planning, or pre-writing phase. Arthur Daigon, professor of English at the University of Connecticut, Storrs, has said, "During revision, both draft and concept are modified through a recurring, overlapping, fugue-like process called into play during earlier writing stages. Words, sentences, and paragraphs undergo continuous rehearsal and revision—the one process blending into and becoming indistinguishable from the other.... Frequently, writers change their minds as well as their texts."

Revising a piece of writing is a bit like working with a clay statue—the material is constantly reshaped until the desired result is achieved.

A Circular Process

As previously noted, writing is a circular process with all its stages interrelated. Although the process has been presented in three stages, a good writer should have every element of the process in mind at all times. For example, after beginning the first draft, a writer may see that the topic was ill-chosen or the content illogically organized. If so, he or she returns to the pre-writing stage. Similarly, if, during revision, the writer discovers unanticipated strengths or promising new lines of inquiry, he or she may want to revise not only the draft, but the original plan as well. Each element of a piece of writing can be reworked at any time. The process of writing is a cycle of continuous rethinking.

Presenting the Process of Writing

The best way to introduce students to the process of writing is to involve them in it in an enjoyable way. As Donald Graves notes, "The teaching of composition or the writing process involves teaching while the student is preparing for composing, actually composing, and reviewing a different draft" (Graves 1977). Below are several practical, beneficial, and stimulating techniques for involving students in the process of writing.

Pre-Writing Techniques

Pre-writing takes time, but it should never be neglected or rushed. Adequate pre-writing time is essential for the production of a good final product. The following techniques are designed primarily to help the students generate and narrow their topics. In addition, a list of possible writing topics is provided on page 11 of this booklet.

1. **Brainstorming.** Students let their thoughts flow freely in order to discover new ideas and feelings. Students may brainstorm independently, in order to generate or clarify their own thoughts. They may also brainstorm in groups, working together to share their ideas or to discover solutions to a difficult problem.

2. **Journal-writing.** Students, on a regular basis, write diary-like jottings about interesting ideas, sense impressions, and descriptions of feelings. Such a book can become a source of topics and ideas for writing. See pages 12 and 13 of this booklet for a list of journal entry ideas.

3. **Idea starters.** Students are exposed to new situations or new ways of looking at ordinary situations. The results of these experiences can provide material for writing. Idea starters include films, field trips, poetry, art, photography, and speakers. Class discussion of idea starters further encourages students to develop their writing in a variety of ways.

4. **Discussion.** Students talk about an assignment or debate ideas to clarify thoughts and opinions. Discussions give students a good conception of opposing ideas and opinions, valuable knowledge to have in the preparation of persuasive material.

5. **Studying models.** Students analyze prose writing that is structured around a purpose and audience similar to the assigned writing. The models may be by professional writers or other students. Examining these models often gives students ideas on how to

approach their own writing, or how to solve specific writing problems.

6. **Interviewing.** Students seek opinions or information from others, especially experts on a topic. The words and ideas of others serve as a basis for student writing. Interviewing can also provide practice in notetaking, drawing conclusions, and formulating questions for research.

7. **Preliminary reading.** Students skim informative books and articles to become familiar with a topic or to discover starting points. In this way, they also develop basic study skills and learn about different sources of material.

Techniques for Writing the First Draft

Writers need a quiet time for composing. Class distractions should be kept to a minimum. Experienced writers can often proceed independently, while beginning writers may find short conferences with the teacher helpful. The teacher, circulating around the room, can also help students who have trouble getting started or who feel "stuck" and need a push in a new direction. "Even professional writers benefit from another person's perception of the work in progress, and beginning writers especially need to talk about their writing" (Haley-James[4] 1982).

Spelling, grammar, and mechanics should not be stressed at this stage. All student effort should be directed toward getting ideas down on paper.

Techniques for Revising

Revising is a difficult procedure for many students. Young writers, in particular, often feel that once words are written, they cannot be changed. They find it hard to distance themselves from their work far enough to reorganize their ideas and delete words and sentences. Other students may resent having to revise because they feel that revision is a form of punishment for not writing perfectly the first time (Murray 1978). Teachers must convince these students that revising is a natural, desirable part of the process of writing. After the students have been introduced to revision techniques and see subsequent improvement in their writing, they will begin to recognize the value in revising.

The following techniques are recommended for teaching students how to apply the standards of revision to their writing:

1. **Conference.**   Oral evaluations by the teacher concentrate on both strengths and problems in the student's writing (Graves 1982, pp. 97-148). For more on conferencing, see pages 21-22 in this booklet.

2. **Teacher-directed revision.**   The teacher demonstrates how he or she would revise a paper by revising a sample paper with the class. The teacher should use an overhead projector or the blackboard so that the entire class can study the process.

3. **Group questioning.**   After one student in a group reads a piece of writing aloud, the other students ask questions focusing on what they still want to know about the subject.

4. **Peer evaluation.**   In pairs or small groups, students critique each other's writing. A discussion of content, organization, and clarity helps each writer improve his or her work. (Peer evaluation is discussed more thoroughly on pages 23-25 of this booklet.)

5. **Editorial group.**   Students are assigned the roles of author, editor, and proofreader, and work together on an assignment. Later, students change roles.

6. **Clinics.**   In workshops, students with similar writing problems receive instruction from the teacher. This may involve completing prepared material or working together to solve common problems.

7. **Tutoring.**   A student who is weak in some area is paired with a student who is stronger in the same area.

Once students have been introduced to these techniques for the three stages of the process of writing, they will have a better understanding of and greater sense of involvement in the composing process. Writing will no longer be viewed as a random, meaningless exercise, but will instead be seen as an opportunity to define and communicate important thoughts and ideas.

Writing Topics

Narrative Paragraphs and Compositions

winning the game
a broken promise
a practical joke
the favorite child
learning a lesson
having the last word
becoming rich and famous
one last chance
playing second fiddle
a suspicion
your greatest fear
the funniest thing you ever did
gaining independence
visiting the past/future
determination
clearing the air
the big storm
a conflict with authority
bending the rules
the real truth
a recurring dream

a moment out of step
an honest mistake
stick with it
stuck with it
racing against time
setting a good/bad example
meeting an idol
something unexplainable
a cover-up
a second chance
a day that wouldn't end
an embarrassing experience
my proudest achievement
the meanest thing you ever did
an ordinary day until
a turning point
my best vacation
the last laugh
talking about it
being a flirt
a Saturday afternoon

Descriptive Paragraphs and Compositions

an approaching storm
the morning rain
a shopping center
an imaginary land
your pet
a mythological creature
a sand castle
an ant hill
a strange contest
a favorite article of clothing
a new gimmick
a musical concert
a shooting star
your bedroom
riding on a roller coaster
yourself
a birds-eye view
a sunset on the lake
a secret spot
the unwelcome guest
an alien
a disc or video jockey
the contents of a purse

the contents of a time capsule
a last straw
a favorite job
a football play
silence
a scene from history
floating on a cloud
the school cafeteria
a yesterday
outer space
Describe a person who:
　gets homesick
　does as he/she chooses
　overcame a handicap
　has an annoying habit
　is enthusiastic
　is clever
　is dignified
　is nervous
　looks for short cuts
　has no friends
　is "cute"

Explanatory Paragraphs and Compositions

Explain how to . . .
- use the microwave
- get physically fit
- make a pizza
- interview
- drive defensively
- pack your suitcase
- use dental floss
- stop the hiccups
- assert yourself
- cure a cold
- go to sleep
- train a pet
- achieve success

Define . . .
- a genius
- an average citizen
- boredom
- a liberal/a conservative
- the generation gap
- sour grapes
- friendship
- justice
- a hero
- your values
- success
- reggae
- patriotism
- Muzak
- video games

Give reasons . . .
- why you were born too late
- how TV affects your life
- how your room reflects your personality
- why cramming for tests is not good
- why a law should be changed
- for talking to plants
- for or against censorship
- for bumper stickers
- there is/is not life on other planets
- for familiy traditions
- why teen-agers should find part-time jobs
- for or against letter grades
- the abolition of curfew laws

Persuade your audience that . . .
- high school sports should (not) be abolished
- the President should serve one six year term
- the electoral college should (not) be abolished
- dress codes should (not) be stricter
- parents should (not) try to influence their children's choice of career
- factories that pollute the environment should be closed down
- minors who commit crimes should (not) be treated as adult criminals
- seat belts should (not) be mandatory
- tipping should (not) be required
- lie detector tests should (not) be admissable evidence
- there should be harsher kidnapping penalties
- strikes should (not) be illegal
- the Federal government should spend more to support writers and artists
- there should (not) be "no smoking" signs in public places

Other Activities

- an advertisement
- an agenda
- an announcement
- a brochure
- a cartoon
- a classified ad
- a commercial
- a concession speech
- a greeting card
- an epitaph
- a joke
- a magazine article
- a movie review
- an obituary
- a resumé
- a tongue twister
- a tall tale
- a criticism of a work of art
- a news analysis
- jacket notes (book, album)

Journal Starters

Write a paragraph triggered by one of the following words or phrases:

loneliness	cruelty	love	faith
peace	ambition	hope	joy
pride	need	despair	confidence

I wish I could trade places with:
   my mom/dad/brother/sister
   someone in the year 2050
   someone from the past
   a classmate (friend)
   an animal
   the President

What happens to . . .
   an empty tin can
   a leftover in a refrigerator
   a child's toys
   last year's calendar
   a sock (or glove) that has lost its mate

Begin a journal entry with one of the following phrases:
   If I could change one thing about myself, I would _____.
   What most people don't know about me is _____.
   I admire people who _____.
   I don't like people who _____.
   My biggest problem this week is _____.
   The best thing that has happened recently is _____.

What if . . .
   giraffes had short necks
   I were suddenly the oldest/youngest/only child in my family
   there were no television
   the telephone hadn't been invented
   the average human life span was 175 years

React to these quotations:
   1. "Give me a fish, and I will eat for today; teach me to fish, and I will eat for the rest of my life." Ancient Proverb
   2. "Keep away from people who try to belittle your ambitions. Small people always do that, but the really great make you feel that you, too, can become great." Mark Twain
   3. "It is easy to be brave from a safe distance." Aesop
   4. "There can be no real freedom without the freedom to fail." Eric Hoffer
   5. "Genius is one percent inspiration and ninety-nine per cent perspiration." Thomas Alva Edison
   6. "Knowledge is power." Francis Bacon
   7. "I never found the companion that was so companionable as solitude." Henry David Thoreau

Writing Instruction in the Classroom

Although understanding the process of writing is important to writing instruction, it is not in itself the key to successful teaching. The teacher must also learn how to structure the writing class as a whole.

Lucile Vaughan Payne, teacher, editor, and author of *The Lively Art of Writing*, has described the necessary elements of an effective writing program. She has said that one of the essentials "is that the course follow a logical sequence in the development of writing skills" (Payne). Similarly, Irene Gaskins of Benchmark School has concluded from her experiences in teaching writing that "Writing skills must be learned consciously in a formal and structured program" (Gaskins). What must a teacher do to create such a program? Some guidelines are presented below.

Classroom Atmosphere

Writing is best learned in a structured, yet encouraging and supportive workshop atmosphere in which students know that writing is taken seriously (Graves 1982, pages 33-42; Koch; Beaven; Gaskins). Such an atmosphere can be created in part by the teacher's positive attitude toward writing in general, and toward the students' writing efforts in particular. There are also additional measures a teacher can take to ensure a positive and purposeful program for the teaching of writing:

1. *Establish a physical environment conducive to writing.* Arrange desks in a variety of ways to accommodate each phase in the writing process—perhaps arranged in a circle for pre-writing discussions, separated for writing the first draft, and set up in small groups for revising. Designate one corner of the room as an area for student-teacher conferences. (Conferences will be discussed more fully on pages 21-22 of this booklet.) Use bulletin boards to display student writing. See Donald Murray's book *A Writer Teaches Writ-*

ing for further discussion of an effective physical environment for writing.

2. *Let the students write, and write often.* The importance of writing frequently cannot be over-emphasized. As Donald Murray has said, "The student must learn through a private discovery of writing problems and their solution. He cannot only talk about written writing, or study the principles of writing, the student must also work with his own pen and his own mind, suffering the experience of writing until he is able, on his own, to identify the problem in a job of writing, choose an efficient solution, and use it with a craftsman's skill. To learn to write, the student must first be a writer" (Murray 1968).

To provide students with the practice they need to develop as writers, set regular amounts of time aside, on a daily basis if possible, for composition.

3. *Relate writing assignments to other class experiences.* As stated earlier, writing must be perceived as communication. To facilitate this understanding, it is suggested that the teacher tie writing assignments in to events that happened to members of the class, or to topics that the class is studying in other subject areas. It is important that the assignment be connected in some way with an event that justifies and gives purpose to writing (Daigon).

4. *Provide constant feedback.* Jack Hailey, speaking for the California Writing Project, stated that "Mere writing does not teach writing; the act of writing alone and increasing the number of writing opportunities fail to bring significant improvement in writing skill. I encourage all teachers to teach composition consciously, and I discourage those satisfied with students making regular journal entries or writing daily with no accompanying instruction, discussion, conferences, etc." (Hailey 1978). Lucile Vaughn Payne supports this comment when she states "It is not enough to give students time to practice writing; without guidance they will simply write in circles." Thoughtful evaluation, therefore, is necessary in any good writing program. It may take the form of teacher, peer, or self-evaluation. (For further discussion on evaluation, see pages 19-34 of this booklet.)

5. *Find something positive to say about each student's work.* Writers put part of themselves into everything they write. In fact, it

has been said that "a writer is a person with his skin off" (Graves 1978, p. 7). Writers must feel that someone appreciates their efforts in order to gain the confidence to try again. Therefore, make certain that a part of your response to student work is positive reinforcement of ideas or presentation.

6. *Be aware that growth in writing is erratic.* As students experiment with new ideas or techniques, they often seem to forget skills they have already learned. According to Piaget's theory of assimilation and accommodation (McCraig 1981), a mastered skill is not as important to the learner as the one he or she is currently working on. Therefore, student writing may temporarily appear to move backwards before it improves. Expect backsliding and compensate for it by reteaching basic skills in new and challenging situations.

7. *Be a writer yourself.* This is one of the best things a teacher can do in order to create a good atmosphere for writing. Donald Graves has said, "Seldom do people teach well what they do not practice themselves" (Graves 1978, p. 15). In other words, in order to teach writing successfully, we must be experiencing the rewards and frustrations of it ourselves. Frank Smith, Lansdowne Professor of Language in Education at the University of Victoria, maintains that students "will learn to write and to enjoy writing only in the presence of teachers (or other adults) who themselves write and enjoy writing." And Donald Murray feels strongly that teachers should "have recently experienced firsthand the terror and joy of putting words on paper. The single most dramatic change that can be made in a language arts or English teacher who wants to teach writing is for the teacher to write with the students" (Murray 1978).

The practical application of these statements is relatively simple. Write regularly on topics of interest to you. In the course of your writing, you'll encounter the same problems your students are dealing with. Knowing what they're going through will help you to understand their difficulties and will give you more authority in suggesting ways to overcome those problems.

Share with the students your experiences with the process of writing. Discuss the options you have chosen from, and your confusion in getting started. Write along with the students. Then revise your paper in class so that students can study your revision techniques and see that you have many of the same writing problems they do.

By sharing your writing with your students, you show them that experienced writers have difficulties too. You also make them aware that writing is hard work. When they realize that problems and numerous revisions are an accepted part of the process, they will feel more comfortable with their own writing struggles.

8. *Allow students to share their writing.* Once students complete a draft or final copy of a piece of writing, it is important that they be given opportunities to share their work with others, besides the teacher. This new audience can be family members, friends, classmates, or the general public—anyone who will provide "some kind of feedback other than red marks" (Moffett 1983). In other words, a writer needs an audience who will respond to the message rather than the mechanics.

Guided by the response of readers, students grow in an awareness of how others react to their writing. They learn to spot weaknesses that may have given their readers trouble with previous papers. They also learn what techniques are effective and begin to consciously incorporate them. Finally, sharing writing provides the motivation many students need to complete their revision and proofreading. Instead of being just another classroom exercise, writing takes on a greater importance when writers know an audience will read it (Kirby and Liner).

The following techniques are suggested for sharing student writing:

a. **Class booklet.** The teacher or the students themselves choose the best compositions each individual has produced and compile them in a booklet. The booklet is then reproduced so each class member receives a copy. Students are encouraged to show the books to friends and family, thus ensuring a wide reading audience.

b. **Individual booklet.** At regular intervals, each student's best writing is collected in a booklet. It is then made available for circulation among class members.

c. **Bulletin board display.** One bulletin board is used to display student writing.

d. **Oral readings.** Periodically, students may do individual or group readings of compositions, poems, or plays that they have created. Students enjoy hearing their work "come alive" in this manner.

e. **Class exchanges.** Classes exchange compositions to see how other students handle similar assignments. The classes may be within or between schools and age groups. Not only does such an exchange provide an audience for student writing, but it also allows students to learn about and understand others.

f. **Class or school newspaper.**   Every student is encouraged to submit articles for a class or school newspaper. This may provide the most stimulus for students to make their work "perfect."

9. *Maintain a writing folder.* Donald Graves and other writing authorities recommend maintaining a writing folder for each student throughout the school year. Included in this folder should be all the pieces of writing the student has worked on along with evaluations of those papers. The writing folder should stay in the classroom, available at all times for student or teacher use.

Keeping writing folders is recommended for the following reasons:

a. The folder is a record of each student's progress in writing from the beginning of the year. Both teachers and students can chart student progress.

b. During writing conferences, the folder is a handy source for documenting a student's writing strengths and weaknesses.

c. The folder may be used as a guide for setting future writing goals.

d. The folder is a record of achievement which can be passed on to the student's next teacher.

Individualizing Writing Instruction

As teachers are well aware, each writing class contains students for whom writing is an enjoyable activity, and others for whom it can be a difficult and frustrating experience. In order to ensure that all of these students benefit as much as possible from a writing class, the teacher should keep the following ideas and suggestions in mind.

Writing and the Low-Ability Student

Every class has students who, for one reason or another, have more difficulty writing than the rest. These students present a special challenge to the writing teacher.

Often, poor writers suffer from low self-esteem. They have experienced failure in other classes and expect failure in writing. They are so discouraged that they don't even want to try to write.

In addition, because many of their experiences with teachers have been negative, these students do not trust teachers. They can be deeply hurt by negative comments and know that in a writing class they are especially vulnerable to criticism. Thus, they eye the writing teacher warily.

The teacher of low-ability students must therefore make special efforts to gain their trust and enthusiasm. Since these students expect rejection and failure, they must be provided with a trusting, accepting, secure atmosphere in order to write. If such an atmosphere is not created, the low-ability students give up on writing and forfeit the unique benefits writing offers them. For, in a writing class, everyone's ideas are valuable. In addition, each student has an equal chance to improve in writing skill. Every writer can achieve success at his or her own level.

To create the positive atmosphere these students need, the teacher must first believe that everyone needs to communicate, and that all students have ideas worth expressing. Once this is achieved, the following suggestions can further enhance teaching.

1. To motivate low-ability students to express their thoughts, listen and respond to the meanings in their writing. It is a great temptation for the teacher to ignore content and mark up a barely readable paper full of grammatical, mechanical, and spelling errors. Such a response, however, will only discourage these students from trying again. Let the writers know instead that what they have to say is important, and that you are interested in hearing their ideas.

2. Provide one-to-one help at critical stages, such as choosing a topic, getting started on the first draft, and beginning revision.

3. Have the students use a section of their writing folders to list the correct spelling of difficult words that are used frequently, and to record possible topics for future writing.

4. Encourage the students to write on subjects about which they have personal knowledge. Writing as "experts," they will then approach the assignment with more confidence and a sense of authority. They may also have the unusual and satisfying experience of being more knowledgeable than you are about a subject.

5. Invite comments and suggestions from the students during conferences. Low-ability students are accustomed to situations in which those in authority speak to them but don't listen to their

ideas or expect a response from them. Force these students to talk about their writing by asking questions and waiting for a reply. Don't let occasional long silences before answers make you uncomfortable. When the student realizes that you really do want to hear his or her ideas and opinions, that student will begin to speak more freely.

6. Be direct and specific in your suggestions for revision. These students need help in seeing their options. Make sure, however, that they understand the *reasons* for what you suggest.

7. Concentrate on only one manageable problem at a time, such as unrelated ideas or poor organization. Be sure to check progress on that problem in the next piece of writing.

8. Point out positive accomplishments whenever possible. If an idea is particularly good, or a phrase exceptionally well worded, comment on it. Sharing a well-done paper or idea with the rest of the class will also help boost a sagging ego.

Writing and the High-Ability Student

Special techniques must also be used when teaching writing to high-ability students. Although most teachers assume that the more gifted writer needs less help, this is not true. High-ability students have their own unique problems.

Talented students are usually creative and highly imaginative. This may mean, however, that they have more ideas than they know what to do with. For example, high-ability students can usually think of a great number of possible topics for writing, but they often find the wealth of possibilities confusing and distracting. They may fall into the habit of switching from topic to topic as new and interesting ideas present themselves.

Another factor that contributes to the problems of high-ability students is that they are accustomed to success without a great deal of effort. Because of this record of success on the first attempt, revising in particular may seem pointless and unnecessary to them. It may even appear to be an admission of failure.

On the other hand, while high-ability students see no use in revising, they may be quite critical of their own work. They are often avid readers and tend to compare their writing efforts with the works of published authors. By contrast, they will see their own work as inadequate. Having little patience with their own "weaknesses," they may become frustrated.

The writing teacher is in an ideal position to make use of the creativity and high standards of high-ability students. First of all, writing provides an outlet for originality, imagination, and talent, even as it satisfies the need to communicate. Writing also provides a way to structure and discipline thinking. And, unlike other subjects in which the gifted or talented student is often held back by slower students, writing allows each student to move ahead at his or her own pace.

These suggestions may be useful for the teacher of high-ability students:

1. Hold individual pre-writing conferences with students to discuss the chosen topic and how to limit and develop it. If students understand how their topic can be handled from the outset, they will be less likely to jump from topic to topic.

2. Hold special coaching sessions for particularly talented writers. Present them with more advanced concepts and techniques.

3. Do not restrict these students to the exact requirements of an assignment. Allow them to experiment with ideas or styles.

4. In conferences, emphasize that revising is not an admission of error, but simply a means of refinement. Point out exactly how revisions have improved their work. Peer group conferences before and after revision will also help demonstrate this point.

5. Schedule group work to show high-ability students how others have handled the writing assignment. Comparing their own writing to other students' writing instead of the work of professional writers will help them set more realistic standards.

6. For those students who insist on perfection and resist making a final copy, set strict time limits to help them set reasonable goals.

Writing and the Special Student

Many classrooms today contain at least a few students with special language problems or needs. Most of these students fall into one of three main groups: students with learning disabilities (LD), students for whom English is a second language (ESL), and speakers of a nonstandard dialect (ND). These students may have average to above average intelligence, but because of their special needs they often lag behind the rest of the class in the development of writing skills.

This problem can be dealt with, however. If managed carefully, the writing classroom can be an ideal learning situation for students who need extra help. Through the effective use of techniques such as those described on page 19 of this booklet, students can work at their own pace while getting the individual attention and additional help they need. The following strategies may also prove helpful:

1. Have students keep a journal in which they record their feelings, ideas, and experiences in whatever style is natural and comfortable. This will allow students to become comfortable with the idea of expressing ideas in written form and will eliminate the tension associated with trying to make writing "correct."

2. Allow students to explore ideas orally, with the teacher or in small groups, in order to clarify their thoughts before they attempt to convert them to written form. In this way, students will learn to separate the process of developing ideas from the more mechanical act of recording them.

3. In writing, as in any form of communication, the priorities should be placed on being understood. To that end, help students concentrate on the expression and organization of ideas, rather than on the subtleties of audience, tone, mood, and similar refinements best left to the more experienced writer.

4. Give one grade for content and one for mechanics so that students will receive credit for good ideas in spite of mechanical shortcomings.

5. Encourage students to work in pairs or small groups. If possible, pair ESL and NSD students with students fluent in standard English, and LD students with writers whose strengths complement their weaknesses. Allowing students to work through their assignments with other writers before proceeding independently will allow them to gain enough practice and confidence to attempt writing on their own.

6. Encourage frequent writing. Because writing is intrinsic to the acquisition of other skills, writing practice will also improve the speed with which these students can learn and express themselves in all areas, both in and out of school.

Evaluation

Reasons for Evaluation

James Moffett, a respected writing authority and author of a *A Student Centered Arts Curriculum, Grades K-13*, has said, "In learning to use language, the only kind of feedback available to us is human response" (Moffett 1968, pp. 188-189). When we apply his idea to writing, we see that, in order to grow in writing ability, students need the feedback of evaluation.

Evaluation does not merely mean marking all the places where the writer went wrong—awkward phrasing, illogical presentation, improper usage, faulty mechanics. The student who receives a marked-up paper filled with vague, negative comments is understandably discouraged. Furthermore, this type of correction, used exclusively, is simply not effective. According to Ellen Nold, director of the Communications Project of the School of Engineering at Stanford University, research has found no correlation between the quantity of correction and improvement in writing.

Evaluation can, however, be educationally valuable. Just prior to revision, it can provide the writer with a needed response to a piece of writing. At this point in the writing process, evaluation can show students the areas that need improvement and help them to sort out problems and clarify ideas. Evaluation can also illuminate the writer's strengths and weaknesses, thereby aiding in goal-setting for future writing (Beaven).

Evaluation, then, is valuable and necessary. But who should do the evaluating? And given the amount of writing students are expected to complete, how can evaluation be made practical? A look both at evaluators and types of evaluation may provide some answers.

Evaluators

There are three main types of evaluators for any piece of writing. Naturally, the teacher is one. In the traditional classroom the teacher has total responsibility for evaluating papers. But teacher evaluation, while it can be effective, is also time-consuming, especially when one considers the number of students each teacher is responsible for. Another drawback to the exclusive use of teacher evaluation is that the evaluation by one person only—the teacher—may result in a limited, fairly narrow range of responses.

Therefore, to evaluate more effectively, the teacher should supplement his or her own comments by involving the students themselves in the evaluation process (Beaven, Koch). This can be done by putting students in the roles of self-evaluators and peer evaluators. In addition to making it possible to evaluate many writing assignments on a regular basis, student involvement promotes in young writers an independence in writing, a greater awareness of audience, and an appreciation for individual personal voice (Beaven).

This combination of evaluators must be developed gradually. In the beginning of the year, teacher evaluation is effective in letting students know what is expected of them and how evaluation is conducted. As the year continues, however, students will begin to internalize teacher suggestions and standards and should be allowed to take part in the evaluation process through both self- and peer evaluation.

Teacher Evaluation

A student's first source for learning the standards of good writing is the teacher. In general, teacher evaluation can take the form of written comments on the students' papers or oral writing conferences.

Written comments on a composition should be specific and understandable (Nold, Odell, Hailey). Teachers should not, however, correct errors on the paper—correction is the writer's job. Comments should instead guide the students toward revising and correcting their own papers. Donald Murray quotes a Chinese proverb which can serve as a rationale for student correction of their own work.

> I hear . . . and I forget.
> I see . . . and I remember.
> I do . . . and I understand.

For a more complete discussion of written evaluation, see "Types of Evaluation" on pages 25-34 of this booklet.

Written comments should be supplemented by writing conferences (Graves 1983; Murray 1968; Hailey 1978, p. 57; Haley-James[2,4]). In a writing conference, which can be initiated by either teacher or student, the teacher can discuss a piece of writing, answer questions, point out strengths, or offer suggestions for improvement. By talking over students' papers with them individually, the teacher also finds out students' own perceptions of their work, their ideas, and themselves. An atmosphere of trust and understanding can grow from such a supportive, non-threatening discussion, and teacher and student can work together to set realistic goals.

Writing conferences with the teacher should center around a piece a writer is doing or has done for an assignment (Murray 1968, pp. 150-151). During the conference, the teacher can answer questions and help solve writing problems. In addition, Mary H. Beaven of Virginia Commonwealth University suggests three types of comments that are appropriate for writing conferences:

1) the teacher asks for more information about the content of the paper
2) the teacher restates or mirrors the student's ideas
3) the teacher shares experiences in which he or she felt or acted the same way as the student

Comments made during conferences should deal primarily with content, and be treated in a positive way, reinforcing particularly effective writing (Graves 1983). The teacher should concentrate on only one or two problems in the writing and should check on the progress in that area in the next conference.

Donald Graves suggests that conference procedures be consistent and predictable (Graves 1981, pp. 96-147). Students should prepare for conferences, bringing their questions as well as their papers. In a writing conference, questions from students might deal with problems of content or process that they cannot solve by themselves. Teacher questions should help students focus on what they are trying to say in their writing. The teacher listens to what the students know and helps them to verbalize those ideas.

The physical atmosphere of conferencing is also important to its success. It is best to hold conferences in a quiet place, far enough away from the rest of the class that the conversation cannot be overheard. During scheduled conferences, the rest of the class should be busy with other writing-related activities. Many teachers also find it helpful to sit on the same side of the desk or table as the student. In this position, both teacher and student can read a paper at the same time and the student can easily see what the teacher may write on the paper. Another advantage of this seating arrangement is that students may feel more comfortable and thus speak more freely when the teacher is not sitting in an authoritarian position across the desk from them.

Writing conferences need not take long. In fact, impromptu writing conferences may take only seconds, perhaps just long enough to give a quick suggestion, such as "Can you think of a more specific word than 'good'?" In general, however, conferences should last no longer than ten minutes—usually between one and four minutes (Graves[4] pp. 142-143, Murray[1] pp. 150-151).

Teacher-directed evaluation in writing conferences or through written comments on a paper has many advantages. First, it is comfortable for both teacher and student. Teachers are in control—they know that their suggestions have been communicated and their skill in diagnosis and prescription for writing problems has been put to use. The students feel secure—they know the criteria by which they are to be evaluated and have been given clear direction in how to improve their work.

Teacher evaluation does have drawbacks, however. Usually the teacher's class load prohibits frequent evaluation—either written or oral. Because of this factor, writing is not assigned or evaluated often enough. In addition, the student writer begins to depend too heavily on the teacher's judgment. Therefore, to foster independence in writing, the teacher should eventually introduce the student to self-evaluation.

Self-Evaluation

It is the goal of every writing program to produce independent writers who can spot their own weaknesses and strengths and work toward improving their own writing.

Self-evaluation causes the students to do just that. They are asked to look at their own writing critically, noting which parts were successful or unsuccessful. Before self-evaluation can be expected, however, teachers should make sure that students have internalized many of the teacher's criteria. To remind students of the standards by which good writing is judged, the teacher can distribute a list of desirable qualities for the particular writing form on which the students are working. The students can then compare their work with those criteria.

As preparation for self-evaluation, it is very helpful for students to be taken through the process of evaluation as a class. The teacher might, for example, project a sample composition using an overhead projector, and then guide the class to an understanding of the types of questions that should be asked during the revision process. Such guided evaluation helps the young writer develop a sense of when information is incomplete or ideas unclear. This knowledge can then be applied during self-evaluation.

It will not always be possible for a student to pinpoint exactly what is wrong in a piece of writing. When this occurs, the writer should be encouraged to underline any sentence or section that doesn't "feel" right, verbalize the problem as he or she perceives it, and then seek further clarification and help from the teacher (Gaskins; Graves 1983). This estimation of errors will eventually become more precise as the student learns to recognize similar problems in later writing.

Self-evaluation is useful for two reasons. First, it encourages responsibility and autonomy in student writing. Second, it doesn't require extra teacher time or class time.

Like teacher evaluation, however, self-evaluation cannot be used exclusively in a writing program. Students need the guidance of a teacher on a regular basis. They are not experienced enough to solve all of their own writing problems yet. In addition, self-evaluation does not provide a much-needed audience for student writing. Peer evaluation, on the other hand, does provide useful reader response.

Peer Evaluation

Through peer evaluation, that is, evaluation by other members of the class, student writers become aware of how their writing affects others. They also see the differences in approach and style between writers and, guided by the teacher, learn to appreciate those differences (Beaven).

To introduce students to peer evaluation, a teacher may ask them to read their papers aloud to the entire class. For this type of evaluation to be effective, two conditions must be met: 1) the class atmosphere must be encouraging and supportive (Hailey, Gaskins,

Koch) and 2) the class should be trained in receiving each composition according to specific procedures.

In order to guide class response to the oral reading of compositions, the class and teacher should devise helpful questions to be answered in a given order. This highly structured format is especially useful when students are not experienced in peer evaluation. It lets them know what types of comments are acceptable, thereby imposing order upon the discussion and, at the same time, reducing possible anxiety on the part of the student whose work is being discussed. As students become accustomed to the procedure, the structure may be relaxed.

Some appropriate questions might be:

> Did I understand the composition?
> Were the ideas clear?
> Does anything seem to be missing as far as content?
> Are there any problems in organization?
> How did it make me feel—sad, amused, touched, interested?
> What are some good points about the composition?
> How can the composition be improved?

To guide their evaluation, the class can also use a teacher-supplied rating scale which should list general criteria for good writing and specific criteria for the form assigned. Problems in grammar, usage, and mechanics should not be considered at this point.

Peer evaluation is most effective when the writer is given time to make revisions after the class suggests ways to improve the work (Peckham). The writer might then be asked to read the new version of the piece to the class for additional comments, or simply to turn in the final copy to the teacher.

When the entire class is familiar with the peer evaluation procedure, small groups of four or five students can be formed. These small groups, working as a unit over an extended period of time, can grow in evaluation skills. Beginning with a rating scale or specific questions, they progress to a less-structured procedure of choosing group goals from a list of suggestions from the teacher, and finally to using very general guidelines for evaluating writing while noting specific strengths and weaknesses themselves.

In addition to encouraging an awareness of audience, peer evaluation has other benefits:

1) It gives students experience in cooperating with each other on a project.

2) It makes each student feel he or she is an important part of a group.
3) Peer evaluation provides students with attainable models for future writing.
4) The process of revision seems worth the effort to students when they know their groups will read and comment on the improvements.
5) Peer evaluation relieves the teacher of some of the burden of evaluating daily writing samples.

However, peer evaluation does require class time, a precious commodity. It also demands regular direction from the teacher to prevent the groups from "going stale"—becoming bogged down in too-predictable patterns of criticism and evaluation. Like both teacher and self-evaluation, peer evaluation cannot be used exclusively.

The best writing program, therefore, uses all three evaluators: teacher, self, and peers. Used in combination, they stimulate student growth in writing, each in a different and uniquely beneficial way.

Types of Evaluation

In order to give student writers the constant practice and feedback they need, teachers, as the first and most influential evaluators, must have a practical method of evaluation. Obviously, if the student will be writing frequently, a teacher cannot be expected to evaluate each piece in a line-by-line, word-by-word manner. Nor, as was pointed out earlier, would such an evaluation necessarily be useful to the developing writer. It is therefore suggested that a teacher learn to use two different evaluation methods—the holistic method and the more detailed analytic method that most teachers now use.

Holistic evaluation of writing is a quick, guided method of rating pieces of writing. Rather than evaluating a written piece word for word, marking all mistakes, pointing out weaknesses, and suggesting changes, an evaluator reads the piece as a whole, considers certain features, and immediately assigns a "grade." The grade may be a single rating for the entire piece of writing, or a set of ratings for the different features being considered (Cooper and Odell 1977).

The multi-rating type of holistic evaluation lists the major characteristics of content and form that can be identified in most types of writing. When the teacher desires to evaluate a specific type of writing, he or she might supplement the general questions about content with more specific questions about such issues as time order and character development in a story, or sensory details and spatial order in a description. The holistic evaluation form may also be used as a guide for self-evaluation and peer evaluation. It can also be used as a guideline for the single grade evaluation. For an example of this multi-rating type of holistic evaluation, see pages 27-34 of this booklet.

The single-grade holistic method is best used to evaluate daily writing samples. It provides the student with immediate feedback without putting an unnecessary burden on the teacher. Multi-rating holistic grading may be used whenever a student turns in a rough or final draft of a piece of writing for comments.

Complete written evaluation of content, grammar, usage, and mechanics should occur only when the student has turned in the clean, final copy of a piece of writing. In this more detailed type of evaluation, the teacher analyzes each aspect of a piece of writing. Such an evaluation is practical at this stage because many of the student's errors will have been spotted and corrected during the revision process. Problems that remain in the final copy are likely to be indicative of where the student's real weaknesses lie, and both student and teacher can concentrate on identifying and correcting them.

Holistic Evaluation (multi-rating)

Using the Evaluation Form

The following forms for composition evaluation may be used at any stage of the writing process, and may be re-used after each revision.

The form should be filled out by the student and turned in with the writing. There is also space on the form for peer evaluation, if desired. The teacher may ask students to turn in only final copies, or may ask to see work in progress. The student states whether the submitted writing is the final copy.

On the evaluation form, content may be rated at any point; mechanics should be graded only on a final copy.

Standards for Holistic Evaluation

Content

	1—Low	3—Average	5—High
1	Unclear, unimaginative writing.	Understandable but unimaginative writing.	Imaginative, interesting writing.
2	Boring or poorly defined topic.	Topic adequately limited and defined.	Well-chosen, precisely developed topic.
3	Purpose unclear, or not achieved in the writing.	Purpose defined adequately. Not completely achieved.	Clear, well-defined purpose. Writing achieves purpose successfully.
4	Writing so lacking in detail that topic remains undeveloped.	Incomplete development. More information needed.	Topic thoroughly covered. Writing is rich in detail and supporting information.
5	Many irrelevant sentences or details.	Few irrelevant sentences or details.	Well-chosen, relevant sentences and details.
6	Disjointed ideas. No transitional words, phrases, or ideas.	Inconsistent flow. Some transitional devices.	Ideas flow well. Good use of transitional devices.
7	Lack of any logical organization of ideas.	Some organization of ideas evident.	Well-organized ideas. Type of organization suited to topic and purpose.
8	Dull, general words, poorly chosen, inappropriate to audience.	Suitable but unimaginative language. Generally appropriate to audience.	Specific, vivid language. Appropriate to audience.

Mechanics

1	Many fragments and run-on sentences. Frequent mistakes in the use of nouns, verbs, pronouns, and subject-verb agreement.	Few fragments and run-ons. Some mistakes in the use of nouns, verbs, pronouns, and subject-verb agreement.	No fragments or run-ons. Few mistakes in the use of nouns, verbs, pronouns, and subject-verb agreement.
2	Frequent mistakes in capitalization.	Occasional mistakes in capitalization.	Infrequent mistakes in capitalization.
3	Punctuation marks frequently misused or missing.	Punctuation marks usually used correctly.	Infrequent mistakes in punctuation.
4	Frequent mistakes in spelling, without any indication of awareness of spelling patterns.	Occasional misspellings, usually indicating an approximation of the correct spelling and an awareness of spelling patterns.	Infrequent spelling mistakes.
5	Paragraphs not indented. Writing illegible. Incorrect headings or margins.	Some carelessness or inconsistency in form. Occasionally hard to read.	Correct form. Neat, legible handwriting.

—From *Building English Skills* Teacher's Edition

Evaluation Form

Writer _____

Title _____

Date _____

Circle one: Unfinished   Final Copy

Evaluation Symbols

1 Needs a great deal of work.
3 Acceptable—could be improved.
5 Very good. Needs no further revision.

Content	The Writer's Opinion	Peer Group Opinion	The Teacher's Evaluation	Teacher's Comments
1. **Interest.** Is the writing interesting and understandable? Does it hold the reader's attention?				
2. **Topic.** Is the topic a good one? Has it been narrowed sufficiently?				
3. **Purpose.** Is the purpose of the writing clear? Has the writer accomplished this purpose?				
4. **Development.** Has the topic been developed well? Is there sufficient information?				
5. **Unity.** Are all ideas and details related to the topic? Do they all help to develop or strengthen the main idea?				
6. **Continuity.** Do ideas flow smoothly? Has the writer avoided any breaks in thought?				

7. **Organization.** Were ideas arranged in a logical order? Does this order suit the purpose of the writing?			
8. **Language.** Is the language appropriate to the writing? Does it suit the audience? Are the words vivid?			
Additional Guidelines			

Mechanics (to be graded by teacher on final copy only)

1. **Grammar and Usage.** Are there any fragments or run-ons? Is the correct form of every pronoun or verb used? Are adjectives and adverbs used correctly?			
2. **Capitalization.** Are all first words, initials, proper nouns, proper adjectives, and titles capitalized?			
3. **Punctuation.** Does each sentence have the proper nouns, proper adjectives, and titles capitalized?			
4. **Spelling.** Are all words spelled correctly? Are plurals and possessive forms spelled correctly?			
5. **Form.** Is the writing legible? Is the heading correct? Are there sufficient margins?			

—From *Building English Skills* Teacher's Edition

Self-Evaluation: Besides the questions on the form, the student can ask himself or herself the questions concerning revising listed in the relevant composition chapter of *Building English Skills*. These guidelines will help in distancing the writer from the work. The student may use 1, 2, and 3 subjectively (or 1, 3, and 5 for the junior high/middle school form).

Peer Evaluation: Members of the peer group should rate each feature as objectively as possible. So that attention will be on ideas and organization, the group should evaluate content only.

Teacher Evaluation: The following standards for evaluating composition are provided to assist the teacher in rating papers with objectivity and consistency. In a conference, the teacher might discuss one or two of these areas in detail.

Grading

Of course, evaluation serves a purpose other than improving student writing. It is also the method by which grades are assigned. Although grading as complex a process as written composition is difficult, the necessity for grading is inescapable. Grades let students and their parents know how well the students are meeting writing standards expected at their grade level.

While admittedly necessary, grades in writing should not be emphasized. According to many of the experts, most composition papers should not be graded. Donald Murray, commenting on grades, wrote, "The student who gets a grade on his paper will look at the grade, he will not look at anything else; and the grade never diagnoses his problem, never shows him how to solve it" (Murray 1968, p. 138).

Many writing experts believe that grading should be done only a few times during the year. They feel that student writers should be permitted to select their best papers from their writing folders and should be graded on them only. At grading time, students may also be given the opportunity to revise a paper previously submitted for a grade. Such an approach may not be practical in all classes or curriculums, but a modified version of it may prove beneficial for both teacher and student.

Relation of Writing to Other Studies

Teaching writing is well worth the time investment it demands. Writing is not an isolated skill—it builds capabilities that aid in the mastery of other language arts skills such as reading, grammar, mechanics, and spelling. Similarly, the organization and discrimination abilities that develop from writing are of great benefit in other content areas, such as science and social studies.

Writing and Reading

"There is a supportive, interactive relationship between the reading and writing processes," says Diane E. DeFord of Southern Illinois University. When a student experiences growth in a phase of either one, it is reflected in the other (Morris). Both are dependent on the student's developing understanding of the concept of word and the rules of our language.

Because of the similar natures of reading and writing, even poor readers can improve their reading skills by writing regularly, as was demonstrated at Benchmark School in Media, Pennsylvania. Irene Gaskins, director of the school, reported that in this program, learning/reading disabled students were taught writing using an approach requiring both frequent writing on topics of interest to the students and frequent conferences on their writing. Both writing *and* reading improved dramatically (Gaskins).

In addition to improving decoding skills, writing enables students to read with comprehension and appreciation. Students who write learn how to organize information and state it clearly. In turn, when they read the writing of others, they can understand how the author went about organizing his or her material and are able to comprehend long and complex passages (Hennings). Students who recognize what they can do with words will be more able to appreciate what others are doing with words.

Finally, experience in writing makes students critical and active readers. Having become familiar with the standards of effective writing, they expect those standards to be met in the works they read. Thomas Newkirk, Assistant Professor of English at the University of New Hampshire, comments that writing gives students an "insider's view of written language. As an insider, as a maker of language, the writer is less likely to be intimidated by written language." Writing gives students the power to make evaluative judgments and to question the integrity of others' writing. "Lacking this power, they are only deferentially literate, they are polite readers. Like good guests, they do not ask impertinent questions" (Newkirk).

Relation of Writing to Other Areas of Language Arts

As previously stated, the language arts—listening, speaking, spelling, reading, and writing—are all interrelated. These studies are learned best when they are taught, not in isolation, but as part of an integrated program.

Grammar, usage, mechanics, spelling, and handwriting improve only with practice. They are most easily understood, however, when they are taught as they relate to student writing, and not merely as separate and isolated skills (Handbook for Planning an Effective Writing Program). James Hailey reminds educators that mechanics and spelling are not ends in themselves, but should be regarded as means to better writing (Hailey, p. 58).

Students must also be made aware of this relationship. They will learn to value language skills only if they can see how they may be used to make their writing, and therefore communication, clearer and more understandable. They are more likely to be concerned about punctuation, for example, when they see that a misplaced comma can garble an important idea. Handwriting becomes more important when classmates can't read an exciting story. Writing gives students the need, and consequently the motivation, to learn these conventions of our language.

Writing and Other Curriculum Areas

The benefits of writing are not limited to the language arts. Students find the skills developed in writing valuable in other subject areas, too. As they work through the process of writing, for example, writers also learn critical thinking skills—how to concentrate, orga-nize, clarify, evaluate, and create. These skills are readily usable in every subject in the curriculum.

In a very real sense, writing can also help students learn content. Writing done in any content area will increase students' under-standing of their writing by forcing them to think through the subject and concentrate on it. Recent research strongly recom-mends that teachers in all content areas make use of writing as a tool for learning. The National Writing Project urges educators to "let writing span the curriculum" (Hailey, p. 58). In the same vein, the Individualized Language Arts Program suggests that writing be ap-plied as an integral part of classroom work in each content area in the elementary school.

Shirley Haley-James also supports the idea that students can actually learn by writing. According to her, writing helps students and teachers examine what a student knows on a subject—through writing, students preserve and express content. In addition, writing gives students working in any content area a vehicle by which they can inform, persuade, transact business, or entertain. As a guide to teachers who understand the value of writing in learning, Haley-James further states, "Learning through writing occurs when teach-ers encourage students to find their own purposes and topics for writing, when they support them as they write, and when they link writing to learning content. That is why teachers who want stu-dents to learn give writing its proper place throughout the curricu-lum" (Haley-James[4] 1982).

The Teaching of Composition in *Building English Skills*

Clearly, the experts recommend a well-planned, formal, and sequential writing program if students are to learn composition. We believe that *Building English Skills* can provide classroom teachers with a sound framework for the structured program these experts recommend.

Building English Skills uses a consistent philosophy and terminology throughout the series, and provides students and teachers with a logical, step-by-step approach to writing. Each book in the series builds upon skills previously taught. In addition, *Building English Skills* has considered recent research and theories concerning writing instruction and has incorporated them into the series. The process of writing is given particular attention.

Building English Skills helps the writing teacher in the following ways:

1. *BES* teaches writing as a process.

    a. *BES* describes and labels each of the stages in the process of writing. The texts include a special chapter introducing the process of writing. Subsequent chapters then show the application of the process to specific writing forms such as stories, descriptions, and reports.

    b. *BES* takes students through the process of writing repeatedly. Students are shown how the process is applied to each writing form studied. Exercise directions remind students to complete all three stages of writing: Pre-Writing, Writing the First Draft, and Revising.

    c. *BES* prints charts listing the steps a student should take in writing various forms. These steps are all derived from the process of writing. The charts can be used for handy reference by students and teachers as they first experiment with different types of writing.

    d. *BES* provides checklists to be used in revision. These checklists are written as questions for students to ask themselves as they revise. Empasis is placed on content—ideas, organization, word choice, clarity of expression. Mechanical correctness is considered only in the final stages.

2. *BES* encourages students to select their own topics.

While *BES* often supplies idea-starters for students who have difficulty in deciding on a topic, the series clearly expects students to make the final selection. Concerning topic selection, Shirley Haley-James has said, "Assigning a topic dampens initiative and discourages learning. Conversely, writing on topics students have chosen encourages thinking and a sense of ownership" (Haley-James[4] 1982).

3. *BES* takes the students' growing abilities into consideration by presenting a variety of writing forms in increasing complexity and completeness.

For example, ninth graders are given the information they need to write a simple, five-paragraph report. Eleventh and twelfth graders, however, are provided with detailed guidelines for researching and writing a complete term paper.

4. *BES* presents models of effective writing as an introduction to each writing form taught.

As noted in the discussion of pre-writing, studying the writing of others is often a great aid to learning. *BES* includes a wealth of composition models. Some examples are from well-known children's and adults' literature while others are similar in style and vocabulary to pieces the students themselves could produce.

5. *BES* provides instruction in other areas of language arts that contribute to or are related to writing.

Vocabulary development, sentence structure, sentence combining, and grammar, usage, and mechanics are all covered in depth. Other language arts areas, such as study skills, research skills, literature, critical thinking skills, and speaking and listening skills are discussed as well.

6. The interrelationship of writing with other subject areas is emphasized.

Throughout the series, *BES* ties writing in with history, science, math, the fine arts, and other academic disciplines. In addition, *BES* shows students that writing is a "life skill" necessary for filling out forms, applying to colleges and employers, and participating in every area of business. Students are thus made aware that writing has a purpose—that it is not simply an exercise to be completed for an English class.

7. *BES* helps teachers who want to teach writing but don't know how to start.

Thorough explanation and a step-by-step presentation make the teaching of writing quite straightforward. In addition, the *BES* Teacher's Editions provide useful teaching suggestions. Each Teacher's Edition (1) provides techniques for teaching the process of writing (2) suggests a number of additional writing activities for each writing form (3) suggests ways in which writing can be shared (4) provides forms and criteria for evaluation, following the suggestions for evaluation described in this booklet.

Conclusion

The teaching of writing can be one of the most satisfactory and rewarding experiences an English teacher can have. In few other areas of languge arts can an instructor see as visible and dramatic a difference in students as in a writing classroom. There, students who could barely string two sentences together at the beginning of the school year eventually are able to compose whole compositions, sometimes communicating extraordinary ideas. These students gain a great deal of satisfaction from their progress, and their successes become the teacher's.

It is hoped that the ideas and suggestions presented in this booklet will be a valuable guide to those teachers who strive to improve the teaching of composition in the classroom. By using the right materials, having a positive attitude, and creating an encouraging and supportive atmosphere, concerned teachers can lead students through the rich and exciting experience that is writing.

Sources Cited

Applebee, Arthur N., Lehr, Fran, and Auten, Anne. "Learning To Write in the Secondary School: How and Where," *English Journal*, Vol. 70, No. 5 (September, 1981), 78–82.

Beaven, Mary H. "Individualized Goal Setting, Self-Evaluation, and Peer Evaluation," *Evaluating Writing: Describing, Measuring, Judging*, ed. Charles Cooper and Lee Odell, 135–156. Urbana, Illinois: NCTE, 1977.

Bissex, Glenda L. "Growing Writers in Classrooms," *Language Arts*, Vol. 58, No. 7 (October, 1981), 785–792.

Boiarsky, Carolyn. "Prewriting Is the Essence of Writing," *English Journal*, Vol. 71, No. 4 (April, 1982), 44–47.

Brown, Rexford. "National Assessment Findings in the Language Arts," *English Journal*, Vol. 72, No. 3 (March, 1983), 106–109.

Chomsky, Carol. "Write First, Read Later," *Childhood Education*, Vol. 47 (1971), 296–299.

Clay, M. M. *The Early Detection of Reading Difficulties*. Auckland, New Zealand: Heinemann Educational Books, 1979.

Cooper, Charles. "Holistic Evaluation of Writing," *Evaluating Writing: Describing, Measuring, Judging*, ed. Charles Cooper and Lee Odell, 3–32. Urbana, Illinois: NCTE, 1977.

Cooper, Charles and Odell, Lee. (ed.) *Evaluating Writing: Describing, Measuring, Judging*. Urbana, Illinois: NCTE, 1977.

Cooper, Charles and Odell, Lee. (ed.) *Research on Composing*. Urbana, Illinois: NCTE, 1978.

Daigon, Arthur. "Toward Righting Writing," *Phi Delta Kappan*, Vol. 64 (December, 1982), 242–246.

DeFord, Diane. "Literacy: Reading, Writing, and Other Essentials," *Language Arts*, Vol. 58, No. 6 (September, 1981), 652–658.

Gaskins, Irene. "A Writing Program for Poor Readers and Writers and the Rest of the Class, Too," *Language Arts*, Vol. 59, No. 8 (Nov./Dec., 1982), 854–863.

Graves, Donald. "Language Arts Textbooks: A Writing Process Evaluation," *Language Arts*, Vol. 54, No. 7 (October, 1977), 817–823.

Graves, Donald. "Balance the Basics: Let Them Write." New York: Ford Foundation, 1978.

Graves, Donald. "A New Look at Research in Writing," *Perspectives on Writing in Grades 1–8*, ed. Shirley Haley-James, 93–116. Urbana, Illinois: NCTE, 1981.

Graves, Donald and Giacobbe, Mary Ellen. "Questions for Teachers Who Wonder If Their Writers Change," *Language Arts*, Vol. 59, No. 5 (May, 1982), 495–503.

Hailey, Jack. *Teaching Writing K Through 8*. Berkeley, California: Instructional Laboratory, University of California at Berkeley, 1978.

[1]Haley-James, Shirley. (ed.) *Perspectives on Writing in Grades 1–8*. Urbana, Illinois: NCTE, 1981.

[2]Haley-James, Shirley. "Twentieth Century Perspectives on Writing in Grades One through Eight," *Perspectives on Writing in Grades 1–8*, ed. Shirley Haley-James, 3–18. Urbana, Illinois: NCTE, 1981.

[3]Haley-James, Shirley. "When Are Children Ready to Write?" *Language Arts*, Vol. 59, No. 5 (May, 1982), 458–463.

[4]Haley-James, Shirley. "Helping Students Learn Through Writing," *Language Arts*, Vol. 59, No. 7 (October, 1982), 726–731.

Handbook Writing Committee. *Handbook for Planning an Effective Writing Program Kindergarten Through Grade Twelve*. Sacramento: California State Department of Education, 1981, 1982.

Hennings, Dorothy Grant. "A Writing Approach to Reading Comprehension—Schema in Action," *Language Arts*, Vol. 59, No. 1 (January, 1982), 8–17.

Horner, Judith. "How Do We Know How Well Kids Write? A Program for Testing Writing," *English Journal* (October, 1978), 60–61.

Individualized Language Arts: Diagnosis, Prescription, Evaluation. Weehawken: Weehawken Board of Education, 1974.

Kantor, Kenneth J. "Research in Composition: What It Means for Teachers," *English Journal*, Vol. 70, No. 2 (February, 1981), 64–67.

Kelly, Lou. "Learner-Teacher Dialogues and Writing That Is Learning," *English Journal*, Vol. 70, No. 5 (September, 1981), 26–29.

Kirby, Dan R. and Liner, Tom. "Revision: Yes, They Do It. Yes, You Can Teach It." *English Journal*, Vol. 69, No. 3 (March, 1980), 41–45.

Koch, Richard. "Syllogisms and Superstitions: The Current State of Responding to Writing," *Language Arts*, Vol.. 59, No. 5 (May, 1982), 464–471.

Moffett, James. "I, You, and It," *College Composition and Communication*, Vol. 16, No. 5 (December, 1965), 243–248.

Moffett, James. *Teaching the Universe of Discourse*. Boston: Houghton-Mifflin, 1968.

Moffett, James. "Reading and Writing as Meditation," *Language Arts*, Vol. 60, No. 3 (March, 1983), 315–322.

Morris, Darrell. "Concept of Word: A Developmental Phenomenon in the Beginning Reading and Writing Processes," *Language Arts*, Vol. 58, No. 6 (September, 1981), 659-668.

Murray, Donald. *A Writer Teaches Writing*. Boston: Houghton-Mifflin Co., 1968.

Murray, Donald. "Teaching the Motivating Force of Revision," *English Journal*, Vol. 67, No. 7 (October, 1978), 56–60.

Newkirk, Thomas. "Young Writers as Critical Readers," *Language Arts*, Vol. 59, No. 5 (May, 1982), 451–457.

"Newsfront. New Study Uncovers Problems, Suggests New Strategies for Teaching Writing in High Schools," *Phi Delta Kappan*, Vol. 63 (February, 1982), 371.

Nold, Ellen N. "Revising: Intentions and Conventions," *Revising: New Essays for Teachers of Writing*, ed. Ronald A. Sudol, 13–23. Urbana, Illinois: NCTE, 1982.

Odell, Lee. "Evaluating Writing. New Assumptions, New Procedures," *The English Record* (Winter, 1979), 14–18.

Payne, Lucile Vaughn. *The Lively Art of Writing.* Chicago: Follett, 1965.

Peckham, Irvin. "Peer Evaluation," *English Journal*, Vol. 67, No. 7 (October, 1978), 61–63.

Rosen, Lois. "An Interview with James Britton, Tony Burgess, and Harold Rosen," *English Journal*, Vol. 67, No. 8 (November, 1978), 50–58.

Russell, Connie. "Putting Research into Practice: Conferencing with Young Writers," *Langage Arts*, Vol. 60, No. 3 (March, 1983), 333–340.

Smith, Frank. "Myths and Writing," *Language Arts*, Vol. 58, No. 7 (October, 1981), 792–799.

Sudol, Ronald A. (ed.) *Revising: New Essays for Teachers of Writing*, Urbana, Illinois: NCTE, 1982.

Windhover, Ruth. "A Holistic Pedagogy for Freshman Composition," *Revising: New Essays for Teachers of Writing*, ed. Ronald A. Sudol, 87–99. Urbana, Illinois: NCTE, 1982.

Wood, Margo. "Invented Spelling," *Language Arts*, Vol. 59, No. 7 (October, 1982), 707–717.